Critical Acclaim for *Free Speech*

"*Free Speech* catches lightning in a bottle."
— Ben Franklin

"*Free Speech?* What about free hugs?"
— Colossus of Rhodes

"*Common Sense? The Age of Reason?* Yes, *Free Speech!*"
— Thomas Paine

"*Free Speech* is the thing with feathers…. Wait — I can do better!"
— Emily Dickinson

"Give me *Free Speech* or give me — no, never mind, just give me *Free Speech!*"
— Nathan Hale

"*Free Speech* will take your head off!"
— Joseph-Ignace Guillotin

"I paid a lot for *Free Speech!*"
— Alexander Hamilton

"It was many and many a year ago, / In a nation by the sea, / That an author there lived whom you may know / Speaking of *Speech* that is *Free.*"
— Edgar Allan Poe

"*Free Speech* loves You!"
— Elmo

"Campbell's tomato soup can't hold a can to *Free Speech*."
— Andy Warhol

Also by Eric Paul Shaffer

Poetry

Kindling: Poems from Two Poets, with James Taylor III   (Longhand Press, 1988)
RattleSnake Rider   (Longhand Press, 1990)
Portable Planet   (Leaping Dog Press, 2000)
Living at the Monastery, Working in the Kitchen   (Leaping Dog Press, 2001)
Lāhaina Noon: Nā Mele O Maui   (Leaping Dog Press, 2005)
Road Sign Suite: Across America and Again   (Obscure Publications, 2007)
Restoring ~~Lady~~ Liberty   (Obscure Publications, 2009)
A Million-Dollar Bill   (Grayson Books, 2016; Coyote Arts, 2024)
Even Further West   (Unsolicited Press, 2018)
Green Leaves: Selected & New Poems   (Coyote Arts, 2023)

Fiction

You Are Here   (Obscure Publications, 2004)
The Felony Stick   (Leaping Dog Press, 2006)
Burn & Learn, or Memoirs of the Cenozoic Era   (Leaping Dog Press, 2009)

Criticism

How I Read Gertrude Stein by Lew Welch, edited and with an introduction
    by Eric Paul Shaffer   (Grey Fox Press, 1996)

FREE SPEECH

Free Speech

poem sequences

Eric Paul Shaffer

Free Speech: poem sequences. Copyright © 2025 Eric Paul Shaffer

Cover and book design by Jordan Jones

All rights reserved. No part of this publication may be reproduced, stored in a retrieval system, or transmitted in any form or by any means, electronic, mechanical, photocopying, recording or otherwise without the prior permission of the publisher.

Library of Congress Control Number: 2025932111

ISBN Paper   978-1-58775-056-4
      E-Book 978-1-58775-057-1

1 3 5 7 9 10 8 6 4 2

Coyote Arts LLC
PO Box 6690
Albuquerque, New Mexico 87197-6690

coyote-arts.com

for Veronica

Contents

Road Sign Suite

STOP	5
YIELD	6
OBEY WARNING SIGNS STATE LAW	8
WATCH FOR FALLING ROCK	10
BRIDGE FREEZES BEFORE ROAD	11
ROAD WORK AHEAD	12
THINK	13
DANGEROUS INTERSECTION	14
HITCH-HIKERS MAY BE ESCAPING INMATES	15
DEAD END	16
DIP	17
THICKLY SETTLED	18
SLOW SCHOOL	19
HIDDEN DRIVES	20
SURVEY PARTY	22
DEER CROSSING	24
DIVIDED HIGHWAY ENDS	25
STOP AHEAD	27
SLIPPERY WHEN WET	29
CHILDREN PLAYING	31
ROUGH ROAD	32
PATROLLED BY AIRCRAFT	33

POWER LINES OVERHEAD	*34*
DO NOT THROWBURNING OBJECTS	*35*
NO SHOULDER	*36*
OVERLOOK	*37*
GUSTY WINDS MAY EXIST	*38*
UNDULATIONS	*39*
NOT A THROUGH STREET	*41*
ONE WAY	*42*
MERGE LEFT	*43*
END CONSTRUCTION	*44*
DANGEROUS CURVES	*45*
BUMP	*46*
EMERGENCY STOPPING ONLY	*47*
MERGE	*48*
END	*50*
Between a Road and a Gold Place: An Interface	*53*

Restoring ~~Lady~~ Liberty

Declaration	*61*
I. Preamble	*63*
II. Bill of Rights	*64*
III. State of the Union Address	*66*
IV. National Anthem	*70*
V. Independence Day	*72*
VI. Inauguration Address	*73*
VII. The Constitution of the United States	*76*
VIII. Amendments to the Constitution	*79*
IX. Pledge of Allegiance	*82*
X. Farewell Address	*84*
envoi	*87*

Road Sign Suite
Across America and Again

"*Li vilains dit an son respit*
que tel chose a l'an an despit
qui molt valt mialz que l'an ne cuide . . ."

> Chrétien de Troyes
> *Erec et Enide*

"Not I, not anyone else can travel that road for you,
You must travel it for yourself."

> Walt Whitman
> *Song of Myself*

"Trails go nowhere.
They end exactly
where you stop."

> Lew Welch
> "Hiking Poem/ High Sierra"

STOP

There is a promise here:

an octagonal imperative,
                a portent of fire in a Biblical sky,
    emphatic, but never final.

Followed not by points or punctuation,
        preceded rather
by an indefinite article of faith,

it decrees a motionless moment: one.

Once done, move on.

YIELD

        I remember the old golden ones
                pointing into the earth:
      to get on the highway
          you must give —
respect to the speed of the other cars present
           courtesy to the other drivers
                 concentration to the road.

        The passenger sometimes reads
or invents the rules of the road aloud:
              "Nod to the other drivers.
Learn the right-of-way by granting it.
        Signal your direction for turns
              or changing lanes . . ."

      look:
   let the flow of traffic guide you —
      letting go is getting in
          as when you drift to sleep,
but it's not "highway hypnosis"
    ensnaring the driver dulled
         by white waves of concrete
    drawing head and hand to the shoulder
      and down the embankment —

there is a price for the dream; every dreamer remembers
   the inexorable price of the dream —

the highway is a vivid waking dream of daylight —
         concrete and speed,
     white lines for three lanes,
       lost hubcaps,
torn twisted tires on the roadside
     (abandoned like the molten skins of snakes),
       multilateral signs in many hues,
and syntactic mystery

"... always know your route,
and watch for signs for your destination."

Remember the last word before the driver
                    entering the highway:
            YIELD.

    The new red and white triangles
flank the ramp sloping to the highway
                as you take your first direction.

OBEY WARNING SIGNS
STATE LAW

Headlights reveal all I see
                      of a tarmac road in Texas —
      red eyes glow and go,
            rapid into roadside brush.

      Rufus asleep pursues a dream beast,
                paws twitching on slick upholstery.
I smooth hair on his great chest,
                      and he settles deeper into sleep.

Alone on the road,
              the only way to tell the sky
                      from the ground is the bounds
      of the horizon circling where the stars end.

            High-beams from the car
light a sign down the highway.
                  The reflective little circles
      constellate into words in my headlights.

All drivers read these expanding metal rectangles,
            yet no other sign would disturb me more.
                  The shoulder black and bare for an hour
as I followed lines blankly through the dark,

and then the strange imperative to the lone driver:
        see the sign,
               read the words,
                      state the law.

            The sign darkens as I pass,
and the sun crosses beneath me through the earth
              as midnight changes days in the dark:
      the only difference is the distance I've come.

Road Sign Suite

The dog's tail curls over his eyes,
and I explore both halves of the night,
    a black sign behind me on the concrete line,
        making my way as I go.

WATCH FOR FALLING ROCK

No one ever watches or even looks
                          for rock in the sky.

Gambling that catastrophe visits
                only the distant and the deserving,
        drivers corner inches from rippling granite.

I can see over the wheel
                the summits of rude valleys
        hammered into mountains with dynamite blows.

Yellow oil-crusted equipment gobbled the debris
                and heaved the rubble over the hill,
        smoothing the earth for swifter machines.

I wonder at the other drivers who know only
                the sky is suspended
      above the moving earth.

Road Sign Suite

BRIDGE FREEZES BEFORE ROAD

A bridge is a communication:
                an exchange between two opposite
                              facing planes of rock.

Space embraces the bridge;
                      temperature controls the passage.
          In warm air, a bridge expands to grip the distance
              between elevated separated edges.

                                above
Cold, wind chills the surface   and
                                below:

        frost completes the concrete reach.

Accustomed to clear, civil highway over stone-boned earth,
                the unwarned driver wakes
                          on a sudden span of ice.

A conversation stills, cooling: words will no longer do.

A bridge smooths with silver: a driver tightens on the wheel.
                Four tires no longer grip.

A road may be an escape.

ROAD WORK AHEAD

The passenger says,
"Anyone can see that."
Instead, I decide it is not obvious.

Ripping down the highway
at extra-legal speeds,
road works arrive too suddenly
without a sign.

I've never driven a road
without finding orange
every hundred miles:
flaming color of construction,
hard hats and vinyl vests glowing
near glowing cones and barrels,

a geometry of building and breaking,
rising and setting,
color of destruction,
always burning
where forms are cast anew,
color of my old pack of poetry
and dirty clothes,
color of the limits of the passage.

Tighten hands on the wheel to guide
the vehicle through the narrow way:
it's done.

Another hundred miles of highway turn before the wheel.

Road Sign Suite

THINK

      a big, black, bold warning
              in a huge yellow diamond
poised on one point
      driven into the ground:
      THINK.

      a poet designed this sign
              in a gray blank glass building
coagulate in a city's heart:
    his superiors could not read it.

      a prisoner painted the steel sheet,
traced the letters as bars of unequal length
           with a yardstick
    he returned to the state unread.

    a highway worker erected the sign
in the dirt by a two-lane road to Death Valley:
    he read the word backward
in the rear-view mirror of a county truck.

    a blaze in black and yellow
              in the sun below sea level:
road and sky dust each other so dry
      the tongue bleeds sympathy.
        Heed the sign.

DANGEROUS INTERSECTION

        Roads intersect at random angles:
                degrees depend on terrain.
Topography determines all about the construction
                      of a road:
      over hills and valleys,
              through mountains and rivers,
    roads caper at geography's command;
            motors endure the toil.

    Every driver must bear the crossroad
                    in mind
and watch for traffic more or less than opposite
              to his own way.

    Often two roads converge suddenly
           in some dark summer wood
    where the bold black rubber skid ends
      at the halted heated wheel.

    Angry drivers curse each other
          at blind intersections
                and averted collisions
while Saint Christopher spins on a silver chain
      pendant from the mirror,
    snapping like a road-stone on the windshield.

"Intersections are dangerous," says the passenger,
          "only to drivers
                who forget
      there are other roads."

Road Sign Suite

HITCH-HIKERS MAY BE ESCAPING INMATES

Each is a prisoner of time or space or both.

Yet Oklahoma warns you.
That smiling man with thumb in sky
may murder, rob, rape you.

He must certainly be your brother.

Prairie wind crosses asphalt in a brown fury.

I drive, unable to restrain my accelerating foot
or explain the extra pressure
smiling blank   lifting a finger as a wave
passing a man who expected more.

I apologize to this soul, to my dog, to myself
speaking to the wheel
raving west in my motorized space.

Southern gusts batter the car like time,
and I do not look back.

I fear discovery of my own escape.

DEAD END

                So the sign read
where the concrete stopped on Ash Street,
                        and in the middle of a week of work,
the ragged kids who lived in the slouching houses there
                        played around the post.

        Below the sign, they played,
down the bank of the White River —
                white only when clouds covered
                          the blue —
and gathered green weeds to wedge in the cracks
                where the wooden post split in the sun
        and circled it with string.

"This is what a sign says when it gets somewhere
                someone thinks is nowhere
        and wants to tell someone there's an end
where nothing stops," I say to Rufus
                watching the kids create
                        the mythologies of summer.

The river floats beer cans and old tires away
            covering shards of tarmac the rain snaps off,
and the earth uncurls every direction around the pole.
            Only cars journey to no end,
                  stopping at the sign.

DIP

        Actually, no warning:
the highway seems even to the edge
                    where the eye disbelieves
                        the drop.

        Suddenly, the infant slips from mother's knee,
a moment of suspension,
                an instant of breath halted in a fall —

        four thousand pounds of flight,
                plus the passenger,
                    the dog,
                    and me,
        hover spinning wheels over asphalt.

        Baby's weight draws mother's skirt snaptight;
raw breath flies down the reedy throat
                        and cries out tears:
                the song of a sturdy seam.

        Tires yawp as concrete grips rubber,
springs recoil, shocks jolt,
                the frame scrapes the lane,
                        and the car rocks a mile.

        Glancing in the mirror,
            even through the glare of the sun setting:
the road's already taut once more,
                      seamless to the horizon.

THICKLY SETTLED

Vermont mountains rounded like matronly breasts
                in the old green sweater,
     we cross the heart on the concrete strap,
           passing another unexpected sign.

Do these fertile leaves conceal such a fact?
        Do people really live in the old lumber
              erected into dwellings in a new wood?
Do men really imagine landscapes in the shape
                of women they cannot love?

Gravel stuffs the throat of the ditch by the side
          of every two-lane highway,
      and looking into that vertical flash of drive
discovers nothing but trunks behind trunks
               behind leaves.

Trees harbor houses beneath banners of leaves
           and trunks later hewn into picnic tables
     for the Fourth of July
         where women awaiting September 6th
grow pregnant with the food their children waste;
     the kids climb their mothers like mountains
to rest on the flowered spandex
          making laps of flabby thighs.

SLOW SCHEOOL

"These are verbs,"
             she said.

"A verb," she said, "can be modified
                      by an adverb
as an adjective modifies a noun."

She said, "Are there any questions?"

A hand waved in the middle of the row
                      by the window.

"Yes," she said.

"Doesn't a verb kinda modify a noun
                      kinda?"

"No," she said, "Never."

Outside, a car passed along the street
                      cut into diamonds
by the chain-link fence.

"Now stop daydreaming," she said,
                      "and listen."

HIDDEN DRIVES

The road is open; the sky is clear,
                      and yet
      this yellow diamond of warning.
Narrowing vision to more cautious sight,
I look twice: observing blue sky, blue road,
                   blue eye,
    a tunnel of sky and earth.

                Perhaps
  in the bushes, drives to hidden houses
            open like green mouths in the dark —
stalking the shoulder rolling backward
  in the odd elliptical one
            mounted mid-windshield
and the circular one
               glancing back from outside the door
  reflecting the darkening blue.

Only when you look at them are they visible,
    blind spots to the driving direction —
                        blinding at night —
  thoughtless bright lights behind,
the mirrors reflect receding everywhere
              the car and driver once were,
  shaped by the frame of metal mounting
beveled at the edge
    to cut the night
           to fit the determined shape:
a tunnel into darkness receding
  like the barrel of a rifle to an eye.

              Maybe
  the past is a gear making motion
           with your life:
underdrive through the universal joint —
    the spinning cylinder beneath
turning that steady hectic thrumming urge
                  onward:

Road Sign Suite

    adjust the mirror as you will,
            and you may see your eye,
but then you will no longer see the road.

    "The outer eye invents this hue,"
        says the passenger
as twilight blooms in the running trees,
          "the other eye understands:
   the sky must be the source."

Glancing at the mirror to see
              the coming and going,
     I drive away from both —
as the highway ahead unwinds
            from the horizon,
   the road lifts gently, bluely as I watch.

SURVEY PARTY

           Awakening with my head on the wheel,
                I rub the night from my eyes,
take my lenses from the dash,
                and the early world grows clear:
black figures on the embankment against the stars
                and blue fading to lighter blue
as the sun recovers them rising —
                      one squats by two boxes
assembling a long pole on the ground
winding section into section.
                      Another stands at a tripod
            wiping the lenses of the transit.
A third unfolds a map
              and scans it with his hand.

      The first crosses the highway before the car
to stand midway between the two
            halves of the interstate
        holding the pole erect:
    Rufus watches him, looks at me, and turns again,
and I remember Rufus running at our rest stops
      loping like a wolf through roadside brush,
           barking at scents he doesn't know —
red fur flecked with gold,
        white chest from chin to belly,
and a black face where brown eyes disappear at night.
   "Rufus Ortus," someone said before we left,
      but watching the dog run
           I forgot to ask.

              On top of the hill,
        the map man hunches over his chart
     flicking silver instruments across contour lines
as he draws or measures or plots positions.
    The passenger rolls in his sleep
stretched across his green pack and my old orange one:

Road Sign Suite

                    how often I forget
         him, wondering sometimes if he's there at all,
and I recall not remembering his name
                           and don't remember what it is.
        Turning his face to the crease in the seat,
                the passenger speaks in his dream.

          Aligning the instrument true to the plumb,
the surveyor squints through the lens
         adjusted to the limits of the transit's power,
                speaking without turning to the map man.
      Pulling a notebook from a breast pocket,
he opens and writes looking down the sight again,
                  writes not looking away or down,
      then stands and waves the pole man back
           while the map man shakes his head.

        The three stand in the sun,
repacking equipment as I close my notebook
                       and start the car
    with a strange urge to name myself, and I do,
pulling from the shoulder into the slow lane
            as the gravel grates, gaining speed.

          Rufus watches the three as we pass,
and I imagine crossing the line from the lens as we go.
                  The passenger sits up in the seat.
   "Where are we?" he asks,
           scratching his head and yawning.
Rufus turns once in a circle and lays down
               with his head on my leg.
   "Nowhere," I say laughing,
                  "Here."

DEER CROSSING

for G.S.
this poem is for deer, too

Would that some god or goddess might bound
        strong and well-
    armed from the brain of some poet
to grant you darkness and cast this spell
            on our concrete:

"Fearless, you may await the bright beams,
      ready for the mechanical gorgon
    the driving of men makes.

    Breathe in the silence as we start
            to see our light
              in your eyes.

     Look on us aware and stand
      still, steadfast,
  to slay us with our own reflections."

Road Sign Suite

DIVIDED HIGHWAY ENDS

This is the way it *really* happened:

  The sun was setting on the road
as I drove through Pennsylvania
      and darkness gathered dust
   in the four corners of my eyes
squinting westward making time.

  On the right, beyond the shoulder,
a high rock face turned before
      to behind us,
  split suddenly in a vertical chasm
   that descended beneath the level
     the highway ran
revealing a red road
    surfaced by the sun
  descending in the other direction.

  Speeding by the narrow cut,
my eyes lured from the light of the highway ahead
  by the sudden ear-raising nose-pointing
      sight of the dog:
  a runner, shirtless with blue shorts,
leaning forward with lightly closed fists,
   sinews bunching above the knee
  as the reaching toe
     found the ground,
appeared running on the red the other way.

  A still moment at 60:
    he raised his eyes to mine,
raised an open hand in a single wave simultaneously,
     recognizing the touch;
  still at 60, the valley closed at once,
and my hand came down of its own accord
   and rested on the crest of the dog.

Sun down,
spitting colors like blessings on the bony clouds,
    I knew the poise of a moment —
dusk becomes dawn but still dusk,
                a twilight as eternal
        as the runner poised in air
                before his foot descends
    to touch the earth for further flight.

        At the truck stop,
    filling the tank, I told the sleepy passenger
            about our wave at sunset.
He kept working his way through his belongings,
        seeking something he wanted
                    but never found that night
    in his dusty green pack in the backseat.

            The tank was full
    when he emerged and stood by the car.
        "No one will believe it," he said,
                    locking the door.

STOP AHEAD

At the intersection in the distance,
the four-way stop before the entrance ramp,
    stands red hair, poise, and a purple pack,
    arm up with a thumb raised.
"What do you think of hitch-hikers?"
        Says the passenger,
    "I've been one myself."

I turn the wheel to the pavement's edge,
    and she bends
        to look in and speak.
    Rufus sniffs,
and she puts her hand on his crest,
        petting him lightly:
    "Where you headed?"

        Rufus licks her ear.
"West, until I'm out of gas," I say.
    The passenger laughs
        in the backseat.
    "Everybody is," she says,
opening the door and throwing the pack in.
        Rufus jumps over the seat
    as she slides into the car.
    "Shall we go?"

Returning to the road,
        dirt spins from the wheels
and dust in through the windows.

She wipes her face with a green bandanna
    as I regain the bright concrete,
        the hitch-hiker, the passenger,
and Rufus scenting rabbits
    hidden in the brush by the road.

            "Are you hungry?
Saw a sign about three miles back.
            A cafe's coming up.
                        Sixty miles, sixty minutes."

            "I know," she says,
looking at sage and cactus too white
                to be green in the sun.
                            "Sure. Let's go eat."

She glides her hand through the slipstream
                                    of the car,
                turning up and down and up
a wing in a wave through the wind.
                            She smiles.

                "Fine," I say,
            "It's almost noon anyway."

SLIPPERY WHEN WET

            Times like these,
   a highway becomes the concrete passage
                  from one memory to another:
     Rufus at rest, his wet muzzle on my thigh
         & the car cruises the cement stream
where chrome fins glint changing lanes,
        mirror of the other bright to blinding
               then dark moving ahead.

   Rufus barks at the wind in the passenger window
as he barks into the clear current
        of the river by the highway in Vermont,
   dips his nose to his eyes
              to snatch the little fish,
     silver couplets in the stream
          bed of stones
      flick fins to spin
   into green weeds dancing.

     Rufus wades to the center.
Water smooths the hair against his chest,
        ripples away from splashing paws
   as he laps the river dripping,
       drinking to drop the level
            for skimming minnows.

But I bathe and rise to gently toe the stones,
            climb the tangled bank to the car
   and call the dog
who splashes the sun to pieces of water
            and scrambles up the rocks,
     knick-knocking down into the flow
       a few small pops and bubbles.

   Speed or slow I go alone,
         away from a glide of schooling cars
when windshield spots of water slide the dust aside
              like now.

Eric Paul Shaffer

        The road shines where the rain rides,
my wheels round black tongues
                        lapping the road flow,
        the slip streaming of the tongue,
        the sliding on the street.

DETOUR AHEAD

DETOUR

CHILDREN PLAYING

We pause by the local baseball diamond.
    Lights illuminate the field
  in the coming darkness,
      but there are no players.

"It actually gleams under that black sky,"
    says the hitch-hiker.

        "It certainly is bright," I say.
"It's empty," says the passenger.

Laughing, the hitch-hiker says,
    "But I can almost hear the crowd."

        The passenger says,
"Somebody should turn out the lights."

    "They will," I say.

The traffic light burns green,
    and we drive on.

ROUGH ROAD

          Rocking along a gravel road
backwoods in Michigan,
              sleeping, I hear
    the hitch-hiker
            speak to the mirror
    to the passenger:

    "I was living with a poet —
an older guy with heart trouble —
               one night
    a thump in the hallway,
          and he was gone."

"A heart attack?"
            says the passenger.

She glances at him and the dog
        backseat in the mirror,
              says,
"A stroke. A vessel in his brain
        broke. He left me nothing
           he said he would.
    So I'm out
        on the road."

    Under the car, stones
rattle and crash in the wells
           of the wheels.
    Afternoon pulses
        through sleep in my ear.

PATROLLED BY AIRCRAFT

          Too many thoughts of men with wings
engender the notion of God or gods
                        turning great eyes on us
              through microscopes focusing down.

    The truckers looking up name it
                        "the eye in the sky,"

    and the passenger points
                when sun silvers the plane.

          Today is bright and blue,
and men who might fly to any height
                      or any distance they choose
        monitor our slow progress on the ground.

POWER LINES OVERHEAD

"How typical," says the hitch-hiker,
"to suspend lines of power in the sky on poles."

Near the construction site,
the sign warns operators of heavy equipment
                        not to tangle metal claws
in the vast web of power above the continent.

"I want power closer to earth
         than black lines of public utility allow
when current flows through old pennies
             and charges for power surge."

"Lines are only channels" says the passenger,
              pointing to white highway lines.
"Are those close enough to the ground for you?"

"That's not what I mean," she says,
              "power rains down on all of us
from the sun every day. Look around.
                  Plenty for everyone."

In the mirror, she catches my eye
         where I slouch in the back-seat listening
with my notebook open on my knee,
            dozing with a pen in hand.

"There's the power I want to see," she says,
         "Something we can all understand."

DO NOT THROW
BURNING OBJECTS

        This warns the gods
                we make ourselves
when we raise signs for each other
            as screens against the view,
     seeing only
yellow paint on the steel
            and not the ground beyond.

Lightning bolts, falling stars,
            and balls of fire cast to earth
remind these drivers of little
       lives rolling through the country
              of California
             all the land is brown and gold
  — trees, beer bottles, skin, cars, grass —

           and the danger of fire rises
       beyond our desire
to prevent the flames
           harvesting the hot and dry
     from earth broken and burning,
          even fertile enough
for the dreams of the rest of the world.

NO SHOULDER

Calls to mind
the vision of a severed head
held aloft by the locks and a bloody hand
to petrify heroes
and free virgins from monsters in the sea.

Driving down the road in America,
the meaning is simpler:
the edge of highway falls
too sharply to leave the lane safely
no matter what the emergency.

The sign makes the road severe
and resolutely less
than my favorite childhood phrase implies —
"the whole wide world."

This grim black line through Dakota hills
transforms, becomes
an infinitely narrow beast
upon whose back we ride.

OVERLOOK

Off the highway, at the edge, there is only desert.

Pink, orange, red, and brown plains and buttes
                             beneath a sky scoured blue.

The horizon is a line and a hard, dry wind
               rattling tumbleweeds reluctant to tumble.

"Man, there's nothing here," says the passenger.

The cliff plummets to the unseen from the guardrail,
               and everything in the world is beyond us.

GUSTY WINDS MAY EXIST

The road silvers and stretches
               in two empty lanes
to an empty horizon.

Rufus and the passenger sleep
      in the back seat.
The hitch-hiker is languid in the heat.

The mountains fade into the haze
           behind us,
    and the prairie shimmers
beneath a heartless blue.

I read the sign aloud, too bored
                    to be silent.

Eyes closed, head back, the hitch-hiker
           speaks, plainly,
simply, she says,
      "Well, yeah, they may."

END DETOUR

UNDULATIONS

        Adam thought the Earth flat
            as he slunk through the circular walls
                of warm green Eden,
        and so did his sons
who paved the road from the garden,
        rolling the surface level,
            even to the horizon:
    constellations of the broken bones of the Earth
crushed into the sticky sap from underground
            glinting like stars in sunlight
                or headlights.

        Still on the surface of the old road by the zoo,
            there are waves,
        solid chassis-rattling waves.
Cars braking make them,
    for cars brake unevenly,
        and the varying pressure buckles macadam,
even the most densely crushed against the dirt;
    soon the street rolls like breakers to a beach.

        "A true straight line exists only in geometry," I say,
            raising my head to look into the backseat
              where the passenger lies.
The tarmac waves jolt the car rolling too quickly
        over the imaginary level of the street.
The voice of the passenger jerks as the seat pounds his back:
    "Waves are the two-dimensional
            representation of a spiral.
    An extra dimension proves that."

Braking for the light only builds the waves
            and jars the car, waking the dog
        who hangs his head from the window
yawning at a street rippling with heat.
    I remember when the Earth was flat
        and God modeled the universe
    from the head of a man

Eric Paul Shaffer

                    wondering at a new dimension.
Rufus raises his nose and ears
              as we pass the zoo, snatching the scent
of a rare beast from a distant continent.

Road Sign Suite

NOT A THROUGH STREET

*The Red Monk was asked by a traveler,
"What is the ring of bone?" The Red Monk replied,
"Inside the burger is beef; inside the bottle is beer."*

But not even to my eye
        does the concrete,
edged by the huge trunks of trees
wavering in shadows and bright leaves above my head
        down to the minute distance
        of limbs spinning from one tree to another
as we pass and disappearing under a thumb
        raised red and bone before my eye
and growing larger again as I reverse my gaze,
        end:
the road goes on until it fades from me,
and I pity drivers turning from the sign
        never to explore
the passage where a rare driver emerges
        with souvenirs of the curving distance
        the road really reaches —
leaves of an autumn oak,
        petals found near a sunlit stone,
specimens of days spent
        in the system of the sun I live in,
        looking closely at the great
in the small in the great,
reading pages in pebbles and leaves
        opened at random
to the lines in the human hand.

ONE WAY

A question of the soul:
We assume there is one right way.

Perhaps it's as clear
as it looks in black and white
but such extremes ignore the extremes
                                    implied,
and after all, each extreme is one way.

When I mentioned this question to the passenger,
he pronounced,
            "If there is one, there are two.
            If there are two, there are many."
And I added,
            "If there are many, each is one."

In my mirror, I saw all drivers faced
with two words on a rectangular instruction
            and a clear direction —
each signals his turn.

Hands on the wheel, I see there is one way:
one way is the way I always go.

Road Sign Suite

MERGE LEFT

> "Our age is retrospective."
> —*Ralph Waldo Emerson*

Drivers dazed by the road all around me
        check reflections in their rear-view mirrors:
the horizon creeps to the edge of the hood
            and slips beneath the car:
    a wave sliding out under
        a wave curling in above.

    The sign rocks on a portable stand —
yet even dayglow orange
        can't catch
            the eye cast back
wanting to see the world appear from nowhere
        from beneath the wheels.

            Concrete walls the highway
        sprawls into the slow lane
    verges into the cruising
crossing to the fast edge:
    red signals crowded force a hectic merge.

        Slow drivers slow drivers
            driving the slow flow
    fast as the road appears when watched:
the horizon leads the steady eye driving
            on the edge.

END CONSTRUCTION

The sign is far beyond where one can see
                          the highway is open:
      narrowing the eye fixes the point
              connecting road and sky.

Making monuments is a physical business,
                and we have built enough
     to challenge time —
               still we expect dust.

Proclaim an end to this task,
                    a time for celebration
         and admiration of effort.
     Work is done: there is a new form.

Amen. These words, as they are, complete.
        Believe other means of construction
                          exist.
      Seize them: build the intangible.

DANGEROUS CURVES

"What's so dangerous about curves?"
                              says the passenger.

Rising and banked for the multi-mile-per-hour force
        leaning on my wheels in the turn,
                        rubber/concrete friction
draws me like gravity around an imaginary center
                against a sudden loss of traction
        that might send me screeching centrifugally
                        from the circling curve.

Even at 75, the car glides around the edge,
                        not even shifting on the springs.
On curves so carefully constructed,
                there is no danger
                        when one trusts the road.

Ascending through the twist of the highway
                        reveals more of the road,
        shows the interchange ahead,
   and from here, I see the road becomes the sky
                under the sun in the west.

As the curve completes its coil,
                        returns to the line of concrete
        straight to the horizon,
                the highway continues beyond,
intimating greater curves
        turning past the line of sight,
                tracing a greater circle
                        through the curve of the Earth
                in orbit around the sun
                        revolving round a galaxy
                turning around no center at all
        and curving anyway.

BUMP

                    a warning far in advance:
the centrifugal fist of earth visible for miles,
          rock fingers fold in a solid punch
                          beneath the asphalt —

      seeing so much so far away,
                      speed remains even
until the blow lands in your stomach,
          and the bumper grazes sparks in the lane,

slaps the frame up blue from black,
                teeth closing on your tongue,
                    jaw stiffening;
          eyes narrow and tears blur in the corners:

            car still on the road,
        states passing into days on the shoulder,
a sudden ascent told in sleeves wiping your eyes,
          and the taste of blood on your tongue.

EMERGENCY STOPPING ONLY

"How many wheels does a car need
 anyway?" asks the passenger.
"More than three," I say, jacking up the car
 on the sandy shoulder of Arizona.
  "Five," says the hitch-hiker.

One drives on four, yet the presence of the unseen
 fifth wheel, that spare in the trunk,
  assures the journey goes on.

  The right front tire sliced by the rim
hangs in black rubber strands of gorgon hair
 around the blank silver face of the hub cap.

Rufus pants in the shadow of the car
 near a hub cap filled with water
  the hitch-hiker set in the dust.

 The passenger grapples with the atlas.
"Might as well walk straight to the next exit,"
  he says, pointing into the morning.

Seeking a wheel on foot through the general heat,
 I raise my thumb to the hum behind me,
  welcoming even the warm breeze of continuing cars.

I count and recount the wheels turning by.
  "How many wheels does a car need?" I say,
 wishing the dog was beside me to ask.
  "Four," I tell the desert. "At least four."

MERGE

        with the highway,
    the concrete way of getting somewhere,
a path of neutral color going everywhere
                      at once

        here and then and there
    beneath the wheel
        a million revolutions
    and ten thousand revelations
            a thousand turns away.

    No matter where the road goes,
           my wheels take me round
the bulk of the provident planet
        to where I may arrive
            to see where I've been:
    passages recorded in the passing,
        changing through the passage,
as leaves turn stem to edge
    in the wild windy wake of the car.

        A destination distracts one
    from the driving —
not driving without direction,
          for to drive is to direct
    your four wheels with a single wheel
              in your hands,
    where all is before one,
    behind everywhere I've ever been,
but going somewhere without getting somewhere
        is getting nowhere,
and drives you to the here and now —
    heat rippling the road
        over the engine,
    bugs bashed against the glass,
arm crooked through the window
        reddened,
    wind rippling the hair

      cooling the skin,
            here and now,
         right where you are.

"Once you're on the road
      you're on the road always,"
           says the passenger back there,
and the hitch-hiker smiles.

        You are the road,
mapping concrete constellations
        where each of us creates
           the figure of a self
    by driving lines across,
around the continent,
        an atlas with an index
           beneath the weight
  of all the concrete
      you've ever driven,
and getting there is getting nowhere
    because getting there
        you find an end no end,
  knowing that you've been here
        and now before
      always anyway.

END

No road can do this.

Try it: follow the pavement to this sign.

Can you still turn
right,
left,
around?

The road is gray infinity
around the turning
and returning wheel.

Between a Road and a Gold Place: An Interface

In Speech We Trust

FREE SPEECH IS FREE, but books cost money, so help a writer out by buying two or three of these volumes and forcing one on a significant other, fairweather friend, or political enemy to celebrate Hallowe'en. If you can find me, I'll pay you a dollar to sign and inscribe your lawfully purchased volume.

As a writer and a guy with a big mouth, free speech is fine by me and one of my favorite constitutional rights. Americans need the right to speak as much as we need the right to remain silent (unemployed as that one so often remains).

For me, free speech means the right to write the truth as I see the truth so that you can, too. Literature is my jam (in every sense of the word, classic and contemporary), so like the First Amendment, I support the right to burn draft cards and flags, use offensive language, and sit silent during the Pledge of Allegiance and National Anthem, especially because, like a President, most of my patriotic fellow Americans haven't even bothered to learn the words, which results in an atonal horror of misheard lyrics, laughable clauses, and musical groaning.

Also, like the First Amendment, I do not support the right to loud shouts of "Fire!" in a crowded theater — unless there is an *actual* fire—or to delusional presidential incitements to violence. Too soon? No matter what else, here are some personal and political words I am free to speak.

Sequencing the Human Menome[1]

THESE TWO POEM SEQUENCES are clearly influenced by Modernist works I was reading during my California education. *Road Sign Suite (RSS)* especially was composed and revised in the years during which I took a graduate course on

---

1. EPS (1955–) is egocent*eric* enough to think that the world wants to decode the tangled strands of his Me-NA.

poem sequences from Dr. Alan Williamson, much to his grave disappointment. Please do not blame Alan; the professor did his best.

We read *Paterson* by William Carlos Williams, *Four Quartets* and *The Waste Land* by T.S. Eliot, *Selected Cantos* by Ezra Pound, *Howl* by Allen Ginsberg, *The Bridge* by Hart Crane, and *Helen in Egypt* by H.D. And maybe there were other sequences whose names escape me now.

The course was a literature and literary theory course poking, prodding, and probing just exactly what these writers were attempting in these exceedingly long, clearly and nebulously connected sets of poems. The theory mostly came from M.L. Rosenthal and Sally M. Gall in a thick, critical, and repetitively-titled volume called *The Modern Poetic Sequence: The Genius of Modern Poetry*, a volume only four years old at the beginning of class and published by Oxford University Press (so I suspected the critique was probably okay) and of which, if I do say so myself, I read a good number of pages, and which is now (today, whenever that was) available used, but still good, from Walmart for $6.11.

Although my gnarly Modernist roots are now exposed (Do not trip over them!), I remain glad at and pleased with these two poem sequences, my earliest and among the longest and intricatest.[2] Since those days of composition, I've written a bunch more poem sequences: *Earth Works* and *RattleSnake Rider*, both in the same book; *The Western Room*, in *Portable Planet*; and *Living in the Monastery, Working in the Kitchen*, a poem sequence and entire book. Most later sequences are shorter than these two, but all are equally influenced by the notion that poems can hang together to generate emergent properties of meaning in greater height, width, and depth.

One vague and favorite memory of Alan's class is the suggestion that the modern poem sequence is a contemporary (!) attempt to respond appropriately to the impulse to *epicize*, to create an epic, and since, like most English words, *epic* and *Eric* rhyme pretty good, I thought the poem sequence clearly aimed at me should become an aim of mine, too, so I determined to create and finish some lines to which I could point if anyone ever wondered whether I had ever ventured beyond tight and tidy little lyrics.

I Drove Down to the Crossroads:
On Road Sign Suite (RSS)

I HAD ALREADY BEGUN and continued to compose the poems of *RSS* when I enrolled in Dr. Williamson's course. I had begun writing *RSS* soon after arriving in Davis, California, to begin doctoral studies. I may have been inspired to

---

2. EPS resists all my attempts to suggest the use of the word "most," when a neologism with -est presents itself.

compose as I drove a gas-guzzling, oil-burning Chevy Vega from Albuquerque to Davis in August of 1983.

When I began writing *RSS*, I realized that this collection of poems constituted an always-complete, infinitely-expandable book. In other words, once the first five or six poems were written, I realized that developing characters, themes, and recurring images within the larger work would illuminate and enlarge the individual poems, so I arranged and re-arranged the order of the poems every time I composed a new one. And I was right: every time I added a new poem, the sequence was both bigger and still finished. As I composed, I also revised earlier poems to highlight and connect emerging elements of the work. As the sequence grew, I invented and organized an expansive and expanding tale of four travelers crossing and re-crossing America as the wanderers encountered new events and ideas and signs from the berm.

I loved *RSS* even more because the prompts were encountered randomly along the highways of America, official road signs of red, orange, white, black, and gold, and I began making a list of road signs I had seen and that others reported to me, a list I still maintain. I am an advocate of the aleatory, a constituent of chance, and a representative of the random, so I enjoy working with whatever comes to hand and to mind, making of those crumbs, lumps, and hunks whatever I will.

Appropriately enough, therefore, *RSS* began accidentally, the result of Reckless driving and navigating without a map or guide, but became eventually an exploration and celebration of the exquisite qualities of here and now.

Robert Louis Stevenson once ventured that to travel hopefully is better than to arrive. I agree, adding that travelling well is the entire point. I like to think of my life and my writing as evidence that even if I'm going nowhere, I'm getting somewhere. *RSS* was my first and funnest[3] verification of signs spotted on the highways of America.

*A P*ssed Off and Half-Ass*d Patriotic Eagle:*
On Restoring ~~Lady~~ Liberty (RLL)

IN CONTRAST, FROM THE start, *RLL* was conceived a multi-part poem appraising and perusing obvious and obscure motivations for renovating the Statue of Liberty. I began writing with the idea that this would be a poem sequence of many parts, as Hart did; much research, as Ezra did; much mythology, as Hilda did; much musical language, as Tommy did, and much outrage, as Allen did.[4]

---

3. See note 2.
4. Hart is Hart Crane (1899–1932), author of *The Bridge;* Ezra is Ezra Pound (1885–1972), author of *The Cantos;* Hilda is Hilda Doolittle, best known as H. D. (1886–1961), author of *Helen in Egypt;* Tommy is Thomas Stearns Eliot,

To answer the question most audience members ask Steve,[5] I know exactly where I got the idea. Flipping through *Time, Newsweek,* or *Mad,* one day in the UCD library, I found a story about the restoration of the statue for the Bicentennial, then already ten years late. So much for a "New York minute." I read that workers refurbishing the statue declined the long and laborious descent of the scaffolding for bathroom breaks, instead pissing in the statue's face while working.

I was quite pissed off to read that, and I was surprised I was so pissed off. I am an Eagle Scout, however, and I do have some lasting hopes for democracy, the constitution, truth, justice, and the American Way. (What? You don't?) Anyway, that report electrified me, and the shock drove me to critique the current state of "we, the people," the renovations of the statue, good and bad, and the state of the union. Oddly, I only mentioned the pissing in the poem once.

Many ask about the strikethrough of the word "~~Lady~~" in the title and throughout the sequence. To paraphrase Louie[6], "If you have to ask, ..." Leaving the question there would be wise, but, hey, it's me, so let me add that I hold this strikethrough to be self-evident — except, where the word unstruck is requisite to singing the anthem or mixing the cocktail.

The most manifest and influential structural model for *RLL* is *The Bridge,* Hart's well-constructed sequence, yet the freedom of the American vernacular erupts from my deeper commitment to the word-wrangling of the San Francisco Renaissance, especially that of Lew, Larry, Allen, Phil, and Gary.[7]

As an interrogation of the prevalent, persistent, and pernicious misunderstandings of American democracy, *RLL* is united in ten parts, each named with a familiar term of government and politics.

---

that is T. S. Eliot, known to his friends as Tom (1888–1965), author of *The Waste Land;* Allen is Allen Ginsberg (who shares a birthday with EPS) (1926–1997), author of *Howl.*

5. Stephen King (1947–), American novelist, best known for his horror fiction.
6. Louis Armstrong (1901–1971), American singer and trumpet player, transformational in jazz, blues, and popular music, as well as in radio, film, and television.
7. Lew is Lew Welch (1926–1971), about whose work EPS wrote his dissertation, and whose BA thesis EPS edited and introduced for Gray Fox Press; Larry is Lawrence Ferlinghetti (1919–2021), legendary Beat author, bookstore proprietor, and publisher; Phil refers to Philip Whalen (1923–2002), Beat poet and Zen monk; Gary is Gary Snyder (1930–), San Francisco Renaissance poet, environmentalist, and noted Zen practitioner. To my knowledge, of these authors, EPS has only had an actual working relationship with Gary Snyder.

Thanks to Lew, my favorite poet, one of the sections is even meant "to be *sung*" with an obvious anthemic tune. I have inferred from fellow ink-stained wretches that every writer of poems must prove some metrical chops to the satisfaction of readers and critics somewhere else, even and especially when that same writer never intends to apply those chops to poetry again. So here, and so there. Sorry, Emily.[8]

My Aptitude for Gratitude

MUCH AND MANY THANKS go to Paul Rosheim, who first put both these poem sequences into print, publishing each separately under the imprint of Obscure Publications, a literary arts press. Equal thanks and more go to Jordan Jones, my exalted and stellar publisher, who typeset both books originally, and who now decades later, and likely against his better judgment (just kidding — I think), has agreed to publish the two sequences together in this volume from Coyote Arts. Thanks always and again, Jordan.

And, of course, thanks to all the rest of you, for friendship and support, even when I lack the fortitude to list every one of your names. Speak up, speak out, speak free! Good luck to us all.

Eric Paul Shaffer
Kailua, Oʻahu
January 12, 2024

---

8. The purportedly immortal Emily Dickinson (1830–1886).

Restoring ~~Lady~~ Liberty

Declaration

WHEN *LIBERTY ENLIGHTENING THE WORLD* arrived in the United States of America in 1885, the massive copper pieces and iron frame were stacked and stored in their wooden shipping crates while Americans decided what to do with such a challenge. Many did not welcome the arrival of Bartholdi's gift. The statue was another immigrant with nowhere to go. There was no place to put it. There were no funds to assemble or maintain it. Even the name made little sense and was changed for our shores.

Not unlike the statue, *Restoring ~~Lady~~ Liberty*, written in 1986 for the Centennial of the Statue of Liberty, remained in manuscript a long time before publication, even a few years more than the twenty-one that passed between the conception and the erection of the statue.

He who wrote these words and the nation in which they were written are ever-changing, yet the words remain true to those days and my life at the time I wrote them. Some of the optimism looks a little naïve now, and there is more irony (and prescience) in the construction of the lines than I meant or could mean when I wrote them, but that might be true of any of us after nearly a quarter of a century (now thirty-eight years).

Nevertheless, I welcome the opportunity to present the poem to my fellow citizens and to affirm the embattled yet enduring promise of our nation.

Eric Paul Shaffer
Honolulu, Hawai'i
June 3, 2009; revised December 31, 2024

I. Preamble

"The symbols mean nothing if the values aren't there."
— Lee A. Iacocca

already Classic Coke cans litter the shore of Liberty Island
cigarette butts, bits of chewing gum foil, anonymous scraps of paper
among melting jellyfish, brown bulbs of seaweed, driftwood,
the refuse of America afloat
by the bow of the immigrant ship unloading
into the multilateral fortress beneath ~~Lady~~ Liberty's feet

for beginnings and new roads west in/to America
the sun paves the roads gold rising or setting
and everything under the sun is new
in the city named New in memory of land left across the sea
and the island beneath the sidewalks and streets

in the early morning jump-and-run through angles and intersections
the crowd crushes between lines painted corner to corner
crosses the street against the light —
all the faces filing past, filing themselves away, arrive just in time
to scorch the tongue on hot coffee from a mug
proclaiming, "DON'T ASK ME!! I ONLY *WORK* HERE!!"

               and my work
                     to write
   a timely poem of current events
                    and my country
         right or wrong
            'tis of thee
               I must speak
       sweet land of liberty
               of thee I sing
  for when we let freedom ring
        the bell broke
                   splitting the lip
  before speaking clearly once
     from sea to shining sea.

II. Bill of Rights

"The dictum that truth always triumphs over persecution,
is one of those pleasant falsehoods which men repeat
after one another till they pass into commonplaces,
but which all experience refutes."
— John Stuart Mill

"beauty is a defiance of authority"
— William Carlos Williams

    authority is always the problem —
                  except for the government
                            claiming all power
      the citizens neglect —

    and I am just one more American
                        willing to speak for all:
    meaning authority comes from the maker's hands
          remaking or renewing or restoring all alone —

        here I will draw my line
    and cross America
                claiming free speech once more
    for myself and my country —

    our language alone can free us
                 in a land of progressive tense,
    progressive in the sense
           of *process*, not *Progress*,

    progressive meaning a noun and a verb happening
                      all at once
    always making, yet never made
        always restoring, yet never restored

Restoring ~~Lady~~ Liberty

always speaking, yet never completely spoken
                                           America
realizing any ordinary moment imaginatively
                                           is poetry

        I claim my own voice
for ~~Lady~~ Liberty is not my muse
        and I make no appeal to her or anyone
but those Homer knew as "the silent majority" —

        I claim the lives of those dying
to preserve my freedom (as I was taught)
        and to speak for them,
                to write now right now
mourning the dead missing
                the freedoms the living refuse

declaring all of these died for me, for poetry,
        for you, and for ~~Lady~~ Liberty
                to hear these words
and I must do no less than speak
        in their honor

        in the ringing silence of freedom.

Eric Paul Shaffer

III. State of the Union Address

"Great men before great monuments express great truths,
provided they are not taken too solemnly."
— Henry Adams

"Freedom is just the ticket of admission,
but if you want to survive and prosper, there's a price to pay."
— Lee A. Iacocca

"and God said unto them,
          'Be fruitful, and multiply,'"
and Americans know multiplication
          means products
so they built themselves

a myth of prosperity
          taking the properties of numbers
          and numbers of properties in vain
from those who didn't recognize them
          or their gods until forced to see

the greasepaint grin of Ronnie Mac, Clown
Father of America, conceals
          King George's wooden teeth
in the face of President Shooting Star
     a visage pickled in the gorge

of a New Conservative Wave
          gathering to a head on the President
ageless and awash in some Grecian Formula
          (probably Plato's *Republic* —
yes, Ronnie Mac would toss out poets too) —

now ~~Lady~~ Liberty's gone green
          and freedom's moved to another state
               with no forwarding address
          deserting her in her silver cage
to lift her lamp beside the bolted door —

"Liberty Enlightening the World"
designed to celebrate the Centennial of America
                        arrived ten years after the party
and the magnificent and monstrous monument
had no place to stand

the carpet-baggers kept their cash
                        claiming insufficient funds
allowing ~~Lady~~ Liberty be raised
                        from the pennies of schoolchildren
who purchased a place to place her pedestal

"a common work of both nations" —
after Bartholdi scrapped *"Progress"* on the Suez Canal
                        and sent *"Liberty"* instead
for, as Laboulaye said, "Progress is nothing
                        but liberty in action" —

the French kept a quarter-scale model
to remind themselves
        ~~Lady~~ Liberty's presence was enough
                and size was not important
though New York's *nouveau riche* did not agree —

~~Lady~~ Liberty's design
        comes from men
                loving their mothers to abstraction:
                Bartholdi gave Liberty his mother's face
a stern, stiff-lipped, silent stare

and Gustave Eiffel built the iron frame
                for the copper garment of the goddess
            and later the eponymic phallic tower —
power rising straight to Heaven
to rival the strength of America's Magna Mater —

R.M. Hunt designed four-square feminine dimensions
for the pedestal on which to put up ~~Lady~~ Liberty
            and General Charles P. Stone opened the earth
                through old fortifications
into the original soil of the New World

making the foundation solid on the grounds
that to overturn ~~Lady~~ Liberty
        the island must be ripped from the planet
                by some catastrophe
beyond human imagination until 1945 —

~~Lady~~ Liberty was the only woman present
        at her unveiling in a man's world
with women circling the Statue in an open boat
        announcing her arrival
with megaphone ceremonies of their own

for ~~Lady~~ Liberty is an allegory,
        her symbols clashing in the nation's ear,
              indelibly legible
to any citizen who looks carefully,
        angling for a national point of view

even from across the Atlantic
        Laboulaye remarked ~~Lady~~ Liberty
"does not hold an incendiary torch
    but a beacon
        which enlightens" —

Edison invented the light bulb
        to brighten ~~Lady~~ Liberty's head
                and chase shadows across the sea —
there she stood over the harbor waves
        just glowing her brains out

after Gutzon Borglum, a man good with symbols
        of freedom in stone
    carved away the copper of the torch
revealing the flame
        for all to see

no one admires ~~Lady~~ Liberty from New York —
she keeps her back to America —
        only from a boat can you see
her design to impress the oppressed
                from farther shores —

Restoring ~~Lady~~ Liberty

     Joseph Pulitzer was one
printing names in his newspaper for cash donations
    since freedom means more
to those who pay for passage from another land
and they'll rally 'round raising the copper colossus

but even J.P. couldn't take America's temperature
giving *The World* orders from a boat
    beyond the island and the land
where *The Times* reports today
    the hard-hatted crawlers

working through the folds of ~~Lady~~ Liberty
    pissed in her face
     rather than climb down the scaffolding —
page 2 reports "The Star-Spangled Banner" offends
Professor Titcomb because the words are militaristic

and the melody stolen from an English drinking song —
America, if we are what we drink, what we toast
    and what we eat,
   are we so easily cowed
    because we've eaten billions of McBurgers?

Remember the respectable refusing to pay even once,
    while others provided the pennies,
admitted themselves to exclusive ceremonies of freedom
    as we, the people of the pavement,
crowded the shore, regarding ~~Lady~~ Liberty from a distance —

and now, we're following fifty feet of Mobile HomeLand
    towing all the comforts they can barely afford
      along a crowded freeway
   (all other possessions safely secured
in barbed-wire rental space at American Self-Storage) —

    lawn chairs, moped, and on a trailer, a compact car
with a bumper sticker aglow in the twilight's last gleaming,
    leaving it all behind with a curse
   for the survivors and centuries to come:
"W E ' RE S PENDING O UR C HILDREN ' S I NHERITANCE ."

IV. National Anthem

"We are proud of our corporate sponsors. The Statue of Liberty
stands for everything America is . . . the capitalist system
with appropriate use being made of commercialism."
— Steven Briganti

"Why not? This is the Statue of Liberty.
You know: Mom, apple pie, the flag — and big bucks."
— Anne English

"Merchants have no country. The mere spot they stand on
does not constitute so strong an attachment
as that from which they draw their gains."
— Thomas Jefferson

"Lady Liberty sells: shirts, lunch-boxes, and bells,
        gold pencils and pens, an assortment of knick-knacks;
an oak Grandfather Clock with a gold door and lock
        engraved with her face and her dates of dominion;
            her gold pendulum swings,
            silver chime inside rings,
        as each hour flies, Lady Liberty sings.
The U.S. Mint will sell you a half-dollar for just $7.50,
        a silver buck for $24, a set for seven bucks more.

Swizzle sticks and beer steins, a gold Liberty mug,
        a bear in green gown and a milk chocolate statue,
big red Styrofoam torch, cardboard Liberty mask,
        stamps, patches, and pins, and green spiked-crown sunglasses,
            that aquarium there,
            among striped fish, her glare,
        red, white, and blue stones for her submarine lair.
Can you see that six-foot green plastic statue in the display window?
        Sells for $19.99. Today, I sold twenty-nine.

Torch erasers and charms (metal and plastiform),
      pajamas and plates, and embossed stationery;
an alarm clock for sale — Liberty drawn to scale
      with gold minute hand, and her torch tells the hour;
          pretzels in a tin can,
            a jack-knife for your man,
      jigsaw-puzzle proof the Green Lady still stands.
If you like dirty pictures, I've got some here beneath the counter:
      Lady Liberty disrobes with Colossus of Rhodes."

Eric Paul Shaffer

V. Independence Day

"Is this the Fourth?"
— Thomas Jefferson, his last words, July 4, 1826

"Thomas Jefferson still survives."
— John Adams, his last words, later the same day

        the reports of shots fired
                over two hundred years ago
        resound in streets and alleys
            roads and highways
        all over America today
        celebrating the Centennial of ~~Lady~~ Liberty
            with blasts of beans
        beer, burgers, banners, and bombs
                    bursting
        to invent a tradition rather than cultivate one
            in a reverence for the land
                we live on
        watching in living-room-size blocks of ice-
                    blue TV light
        a fat pack of wealth and status quo
            rehearsing themselves
                    for the benefit of millions
        overlooking the chains shattered at her feet
                ignoring
            the shackles hidden by her gown
        forgetting a chain
                    is a chain is a chain is a chain
        whether iron or bronze, silver or as gold
        as the streets
            where too few Americans live
        waiting for the night
                to light their fireworks.

VI. Inauguration Address

"Here at our sea-washed, sunset gates shall stand
A mighty woman with a torch, whose flame
Is the imprisoned lightning, and her name
Mother of Exiles . . . ."
— Emma Lazarus

"I must write again to say how much I like your sonnet
about the Statue — much better than I like the Statue itself."
— James Russell Lowell

                                          "Crown'd with a helmet & dark hair
                                              the nameless female stood"
the Titan Atlas was my sire   — Blake
        condemned
                to cradle the world
    on weary shoulders,
his muscles maps of his strength and his struggle,
                    bunched beneath the burden —
after the War of Heaven and Earth
                tore the two asunder,
      for warring well against the victors,
he was condemned
        to crouch beneath the circumference
by Zeus, God the Father to the Greeks,
      who place all their wonders far
                          in the West
      and so contrived to place us here,
keeping their reckless gods safely across the sea
            in the sky or underground,
converting culture to logic
        to justify themselves —

the night Perseus arrived   "silent she stood
        I held high the torch   as night"
            to greet the rare visitor   — Blake

                        with the joy
reserved for great occasions —
            charged by Hera to guard
the golden apples,
                    those tokens of love
            to celebrate the foolish
celestial marriages of gods and men,
                        my sisters and I saw few
who did not come to steal the gilded fruit.

since Herakles, we were wary of visitors
                        for he tricked my father   "round about all
into resuming his burden   is mute"
after Atlas rejoiced to be set free,   — Tennyson
                yet once more,
the Titan groaned beneath the globe

but Perseus pitying
            raised the Gorgon Medusa's head
                        in the light my torch cast
so Atlas might be turned to stone
            beneath the weight of the Earth
and I, not meaning
                to see
that hideous face, the writhing, hissing hair,
            the tongue split as a serpent's
tongue worming with a serpent's grace,   "for never
        my voice, too, grew still   from her iron tongue
where I stood on the last of the land   could voice or sound arise"
                this island once was,   — Blake
            and still I remain

                alone
till searching the West without the maps
            my father's arms
                        now seem to mean
the descendants of the Greeks —
                        in thought
                    if not in thew —
            discovered me here
                    my green breast
the promise of a new world
                        defined

                    "sleep and stir not:
                        all is mute"
                        — Tennyson

            in the dreams of an old one
and guarded by giants
            of new imagination
                    newly arrived
                long ages after
the ward and reward are gone.

VII. The Constitution of the United States

"Eiffel's hidden structural reality is totally unrelated to the statue's very traditional appearance. Liberty is an archetypal illustration of the aesthetic tension of its time — when technology had already attained great advances and power and a hold over the mind, but when the conscious eye was still dominated by traditional imagery."
— Marvin Trachtenberg

what we can learn from the body

    of ~~Lady~~ Liberty
    are the lessons of building
        the genetics of freedom
    a double-helix stairway
    winding up in the lofty head
        standing on the imaginary
    copper tongue empowering speech
    free
        or your money back
    proclaiming, "It's a free country!"
    with every single voice
    rightfully raised

what we can learn from the body

    a flexibility absolutely necessary
    for the magnitude
        and complexity
    of the structure as it stands
        yielding enough
    to remain standing
    as long as the copper skin waves
        in the wind
    flexing on the single-bar strapwork
        supporting each section —

   the weight of ~~Lady~~ Liberty
   resting on her iron and concrete frame
        independently
   and not on the parts below

what we can learn from the body

   a 2.5 millimeter thin skin
       another good idea
   for making ~~Lady~~ Liberty lighter
   and more sensitive to sudden changes
   in wind and weather
      over the waves and the world
   and through the folds in her garment

what we can learn from the body

   more than half the stature
       of ~~Lady~~ Liberty
   arises from where she stands
     and what she stands on
   151 feet, 1 inch tall
       and still growing
   in the hearts and minds of the people
   marking her height regularly
      on the golden doorjamb

what we can learn from the body

   ~~Lady~~ Liberty's lips are sealed
     leaving us to speak for ourselves,
   knowing the wiser part
     of the freedom of speech
       is sometimes a silence
   encouraging every voice
     the conscience requires

what we can learn from the body

   a tremendous concrete intellectual frame
   must be wrapped in the humanity
   of our symbols renewed
   through the past

                        in the present
                    for a future
                we will live to see

                    in the balance we achieve
                    in the flexibility we design
                    in the interdependence we learn
                                    as the rites
                                        wrights
                                    rights of ~~Lady~~ Liberty
                    engendered in ourselves

        what we can learn from the body

VIII. Amendments to the Constitution

"Congress shall make no law respecting an establishment of religion, or prohibiting the free exercise thereof; or abridging the freedom of speech, or of the press; or the right of the people peaceably to assemble, and to petition the government for a redress of grievances."
— Article I of the Amendments to the Constitution of the United States

"We found it wasn't just a matter of cosmetics. We just couldn't buy her a new dress and dab on some new makeup. We had to fix her internal problems."
— Edward Cohen

remaking ~~Lady~~ Liberty is a process
of reviewing original plans
              reworking original construction
      replacing original parts
           revising original designs
and remarking, in an original way,
        ~~Lady~~ Liberty was lucky
to last a hundred years
      with all her problems

but there are changes

          replacing ~~Lady~~ Liberty's missing curl
      and hiring a patinist
to make the color conform

      replacing the tip of her nose
gnawed off by the sulphuric spite
           of polluted air

      replacing the spiral stairs
with more stable steps winding
          to the head of ~~Lady~~ Liberty

>   installing central air
> to control the temperature inside ~~Lady~~ Liberty
>   and to avoid extremes
>
>   installing elevators
>   for those who cannot climb
> to look down on what they're missing
>
>   replacing the 25 windows of the diadem
>   so that visitors may share
> ~~Lady~~ Liberty's point of view more clearly
>
>   replacing the rusty iron bars
> supporting the image with new and improved
>   stainless steel to do the same job longer

and then there are changes

>   now the torch of ~~Lady~~ Liberty is gold
>   gilded 24-karat leaf
> since money talks
> telling the truth in our pockets full of change
>
>   IN GOLD WE TRUST
>
> the light of the flame is gone
>   aglow below
>   somewhere out of sight,
> the lesson clearer, though lightless —
>   illumination
>   comes from within no more
>   for the torch shines
>   only in the beams
> trained on the gold from the base
>
> may the gold swiftly wear away
>   with exposure to the elements,
> down to ~~Lady~~ Liberty's true mettle:
>   copper —
>   for good reason
>   the ancients called copper
>   the metal of love

    for the ore was common
        enough for the coin of the realm
gleaming and familiar with use
    valuable only in exchange
        and useless for weapons:

there is wisdom in the lesson the lowly penny teaches —
      treated well
   ~~Lady~~ Liberty may last a thousand years.

Eric Paul Shaffer

IX. Pledge of Allegiance

"Over the chained bay waters Liberty"
             — Hart Crane

"This is the last place.
There is nowhere else we need to go."
             — Lew Welch

    America, our country
the people and the land around us
                one nation
        indivisible
all Americans (like it or not)
                one American like me
    discovering a free country
right in the heart of America
knowing my country
            is the land I live on
grounding my notion of a nation
      in a place where I can stand
against the flag/
           /rant abuses of the earth
under my feet and fingernails

    WE LIVE HERE!

and home is where you're not afraid
             to get your hands dirty
    in the real work
you do for friends and neighbors —
       a respect unafraid to criticize
knowing all could go straight to hell
          if we will not stand
    for what we stand for
and no republic worth a damn
             unless it protects
the lives of everyone
      who dares to stand for all of us

Restoring ~~Lady~~ Liberty

  finding government in our own hearts
    and no more in pledges to rags,
windy old glory sheets drying streaks of blood,
    and no more in marble buildings
and monuments on the Potomac
where Washington began the tradition
      of throwing money around,
for we need the freedom to spend a dollar
without washing our hands of the smell
      of America printed in green
on the coast where the promise is still green
despite the axe in our hands
    taking the liberty and leaving justice
to some power in ourselves
      and to claim no more
  the right to judge
a diversity of people as dangerous
    for once
      and for all —
one American like me
    finding myself
    right in the heart of my country,
a boy seeking my place in the nation
      where I was born —
  a realm seeking peace
strengthened by a constant vigil of humility —
    a man loving the land
and seeking free companions
      somewhere in America —
    I pledge allegiance.

X. Farewell Address

"Our union is now complete; our constitution composed, established and approved. You are now the guardians of your own liberties."
— Samuel Adams

"When we are planning for posterity, we ought to remember that virtue is not hereditary."
— Thomas Paine

"If some of my judgments were wrong, and some were wrong, they were made in what I believed to be the best interests of the nation."
— Richard M. Nixon

in the U.S. Bar and Grill
            darkness
      the patrons watch TV
while somebody else spotlights the torch
      the bartender turns to the screen
            grumbling

      "This really burns my ass.
Somebody shoulda axed me
            to light that torch."

      "What can we do?
Government got all the power."   says one of the bar belles

            "Shit!
I'm a goddamn citizen. I got power.   mixing a "Green Lady" —
      Like John Hancock said,   crème de menthe, clear stuff,
'Give me Liberty, or give me Death' —   whipped cream, & a cherry
      or give me a million dollars   on a swizzle stick
            to keep me quiet."

                                                  laughs and more
"Take a whole new revolution for you   "Liberty Specials" —
      to light that torch."   buy one, free one

Restoring ~~Lady~~ Liberty

"Wasn't that Patrick Henry?"   says the fat guy
                                                                              at the bar's end

"At least, this can't last forever."   says he with his head on the bar
                                                                       and the rest roar

"Will all you assholes shut up?
                 Some of us *Americans*   a voice crying
        want to see this shit!"   in the dimness
                                                                                                    of dark tables

      I'm listening but beer comes
                         and beer goes
and I make my way to the back; over the urinal
                        is a scrawl:
         "~~Lady~~ Liberty is Madonna in drag."

                a goddess in green, still a virgin
                       in the ancient sense
      meaning a woman running her own life
                      the way she wishes
       a woman with a will of her own

     I'm back to my barstool in time to hear some toasts

         "Here's to ~~Lady~~ Liberty in the Harbor,"
                             says the fat guy

     let us raise our glasses like torches
               to the All-American starless night
     across the rolling fields of the dark republic

     let us toast the fire
                    seized from ~~Lady~~ Liberty
        by the men who bought it
             for the Freedom Museum

     let us toast the hills
                      two centuries ago green
            with nothing but leaves
     become bills in golden calfskin wallets

     let us toast to ~~Lady~~ Liberty
                     whose work was clear
         as soon as the light shone forth

  meanwhile I'm writing my own toast
     freehand on a bar napkin

   let us not find ~~Lady~~ Liberty
     buried to her breasts   on another planet
   in the sand once our nation   as Charlton Heston did
      now run out
   through the strait throat of the minute
     we exalted
       to get us to our jobs
   making a living making payments

    On Time

   let us stand on the shore
      of the moment arriving
        in the present
    of ~~Lady~~ Liberty for all
       for America
   as indivisible as a nation from its people —
    for founding the nation
   endures as long as citizens are born
       to believe
   faith is not enough without actions —
     America
   not a product, a process
       for the making
    means more than the made
   and the made must be made again
     and the making will remain
       the same great work.

"Hey! Here, listen to this!"
     and I read by the bar's grainy light
       over the blue buzz
    and chitter-chatter static ceremonies on the screen

"Shit, man, what is that?" says the bartender,
    "Why don't you just *say* what you *mean?*"

envoi

      over the face of the waters
where the Greeks thought Atlantis lost,
        a wind bears salt
                to the shore,
     the sand where we stand,
            working to see
Liberty Island from the coast of America,
      adrift among the waves.

About the Author

Eric Paul Shaffer is the author of nine books of poetry, including *Lāhaina Noon; Portable Planet; Living at the Monastery, Working in the Kitchen; A Million-Dollar Bill; Even Further West;* and *Green Leaves*. More than 600 of his poems have been published in the USA, Australia, Canada, England, Ireland, Japan, New Zealand, Scotland, and Wales. Shaffer received Hawaiʻi's 2002 Elliot Cades Award for Literature, a 2006 Ka Palapala Poʻokela Book Award for *Lāhaina Noon,* and the 2009 James M. Vaughan Award for Poetry. He won a fellowship to attend the Summer 2006 Fishtrap Writers Workshop and was a visiting poetry faculty member at the 23rd Annual Jackson Hole Writers Conference in 2015. Shaffer lives on the island of Oʻahu.

Coyote Arts Titles

Gilbert Alter-Gilbert, editor. *Pipe Dreams: The Drug Experience in Literature*
Jefferson Carter. *Free Hugs: New and Selected Poems*
Joe Martin. *Rumi's Mathnavi: A Theatre Adaptation*
Lawrence Millman. *Goodbye, Ice: Arctic Poems*
Lawrence Millman. *Outsider: My Boyhood with Thoreau*
    (illustrated by Geoff Halverson)
Elias Papadimitrakopoulos. *Toothpaste with Chlorophyll | Maritime Hot Baths*
    (translated from the Greek by John Taylor;
    illustrated by Alekos Fassianos)
Eric Paul Shaffer. *A Million-Dollar Bill: Poems*
Eric Paul Shaffer. *Free Speech: poem sequences*
Eric Paul Shaffer. *Green Leaves: Selected & New Poems*
Christopher Spranger. *The Book of Tasks, Volume I: Atlantean Undertakings*
Christopher Spranger. *The Comedy of Agony: A Book of Poisonous*
    Contemplations
Leslie Stahlhut. *The Secret of the Old Cloche: Agatha Christine Mystery Stories*
John Taylor. *What Comes from the Night: Poems*

Forthcoming Coyote Arts Titles

Eric Basso. *Fictions: The Beak Doctor: Short Fictions, 1972–1976*
    & Bartholomew Fair
Greg Boyd. *Brotherton's Travels: Memoirs*
René Daumal. *The Anti-Heaven*
    (translated and with an introduction by Jordan Jones)
Kendall Lappin. *Dead French Poets Speak Plain English & Memoirs*
    of a Translator of Poetry
Joe Martin. *Parabola: Shorter Fictions*
Gérard de Nerval. *Aurélia, followed by Sylvie*
    (translated by Kendall Lappin and with an introduction by Eric Basso)
Eric Paul Shaffer. *Second Nature: Poems*
Leslie Stahlhut. *Borderlands of the Heart and Other Stories*
Leslie Stahlhut. *The Hidden Staircase: Agatha Christine Mystery Stories, #2*

www.ingramcontent.com/pod-product-compliance
Lightning Source LLC
Chambersburg PA
CBHW030530080526
44586CB00011B/383